YOUR HEALTH

Health and Hygiene

Dorothy Baldwin

Rourke Enterprises, Inc.
Vero Beach, FL 32964

Your Health

Health and Food
Health and Exercise
Health and Drugs
Health and Hygiene
Health and Feelings
Health and Friends

Some words in these books are printed in **bold**. Their meanings are explained in the glossary on page 30.

First published in the
United States in 1987 by
Rourke Enterprises, Inc.
Vero Beach, FL 32964

Library of Congress Cataloging-in-Publication Data

Baldwin, Dorothy.
   Health and hygiene.

   (Your health)
   Bibliography: p.
   Includes index.
   Summary: Informs the teen reader how to keep skin, hair, hands, and feet healthy and clean.
   1. Hygiene—Juvenile literature. 2. Health—Juvenile literature.
[1. Health. 2. Cleanliness]
I. Title   II. Series: Baldwin, Dorothy. Your health.
RA777.B336   1987   613.4   87–12916
ISBN 0–86592–291–8

Phototypeset by DP Press, Sevenoaks, Kent
Printed in Italy by Sagdos S.p.A. Milan

Contents

What is hygiene? 4
Is your appearance important? 4
Hygiene in the teens 6

Your skin 7
The sweat glands 8
Dry or oily skin 8
Body fluids and oils 8
Body odor 9
Check your hygiene 12
Water 13

Stop those pimples! 14
How to prevent pimples 14
How to cope with pimples 16
When to go to the doctor 17

Hair 18
Hygiene of the hair 18

Dandruff 19
Hair care 19
Lice 19
Boils 20

Your hands and feet 21
Care of the cuticles 21
Are you a nail-biter? 22
Cutting the nails 22
Care of the feet 22
Ringworm – athlete's foot 24
Signs of ringworm 24

Keeping clean and looking good 26
Looks and health 29

Glossary 30
Further reading 31
Index 32

What is hygiene?

Hygiene is about being clean, and staying healthy. Germs find it difficult to live on freshly washed skin. They prefer places that are dirty and damp. Your body has its own built-in system of dealing with germs, but it needs help from you to keep them away.

Is your appearance important?
Your appearance (the way you look) is important. When you meet new people, it is likely you judge them by their looks. Other people are likely to judge you the same way. For example, if you meet a really dirty person, you might decide that person is careless about other things too.

A clean, bright appearance is very attractive.

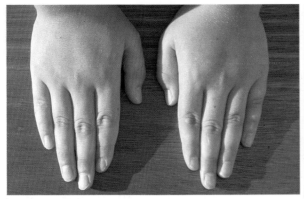 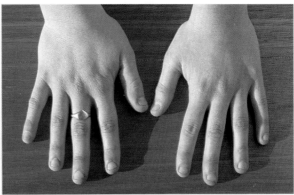

Decide which of the lists below is the more attractive. If you choose the first list, you will need the information in this book. It takes a little extra time and care to brush up on your hygiene. But you will also be improving your appearance and your health. This will also help to build up your confidence. Remember, when people look good, they feel good.

Your nails can give away quite a lot about your hygiene habits. The clean nails on the left give a much better impression than the grubby and chewed nails on the right.

	List one	List two
Skin	Clear, fresh, glowing	Muddy, dirty, dull
Hair	Fresh-smelling, shining	Dank, brittle, unwashed
Nails	Clean, well-cut	Grubby, chipped, bitten
Teeth	White, attractive, clean	Stained, crooked, dirty
Breath	Fresh, sweet-smelling	Stuffy, unpleasant
Eyes	Bright, clear, alert	Dull, strained, tired
Expression	Friendly, interested, alert	Sullen, bored, cross
Body odor	Fresh, clean	Unpleasant, unwashed
Posture	Upright, graceful, alert	Slumped, awkward
Clothes	Clean, in good condition	Scruffy, buttons, missing, etc.

Hygiene in the teens

Your body starts changing in the early teens. It begins to grow out of a child's shape and into an adult's. The changes are caused by **hormones**. These are chemicals that travel in the blood. It takes some time for your body to adapt to all the changes that are taking place, and for the newly working hormones to settle down. Minor problems such as pimples or **dandruff** can happen in the teens. Extra hygiene is needed to cope with these problems.

These teenagers are growing from children into adults as a result of new hormones starting to change the shape of their bodies.

Your skin

Study the diagram. Find the top layer of skin, the **epidermis**. It is made up of dead cells. Under the epidermis are living cells. They grow up from the **dermis** and slowly become flat, dry and dead. It takes about twenty-eight days for a skin cell to grow up to the epidermis and to die. Millions of dead cells are shed from the body each day. They float off into the air, or they are rubbed off onto your clothes.

During the teens, the top layer of dead cells thickens slightly.

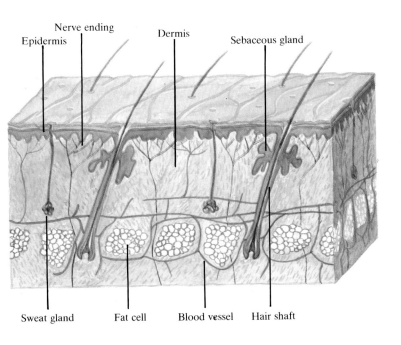

A diagram showing the layers of the skin.

The sweat glands

Can you find a **sweat gland** on the diagram on the previous page? There are about two million sweat glands spread over the skin. **Sweat** is mainly water, with a little salt and body waste. People sweat between 500 and 700 cubic centimeters (cc) each day. They do not notice this sweating. Heavy sweating is caused by such things as exercise, eating hot spicy foods, and feeling anxious or very shy.

In the teens, new sweat glands start working. They produce a heavier sweat.

Dry or oily skin?

Can you find the **sebaceous glands**? They make an oil called **sebum**. Sebum flows to the top of the skin along each tiny hair. It keeps the skin smooth, supple and soft. It keeps the hair well-oiled and glossy. Some people naturally make more sebum than others.

For a while in the teens you may make too much or too little sebum.

Body fluids and oils

Special fluids and oils are made to protect the openings of the body. Tears wash the eyes, keeping them clean and damp. Wax oils the ears, and traps any dirt. Mucus, a slippery fluid, keeps the mouth, nose and air passages clean. The genitals (the sex organs) have their own fluids and oils to keep them clean.

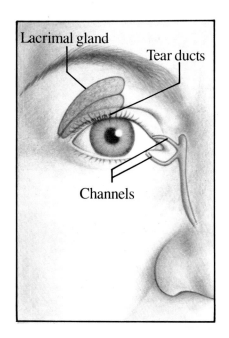

The lacrimal gland produces tears to keep the eye clean and moist. Tears travel through tear ducts onto the surface of the eye and drain away through channels in the corner into the nose.

Body fluids and oils not only keep the openings clean, they also keep them comfortably damp.

Vigorous exercise causes heavy sweating. Sweat is a mixture of water and waste products from the body.

Body odor

Sweat, even underarm sweat, is pleasant when it is fresh – a special "you" smell. All the body fluids and oils smell nice when they are fresh. But if they remain on the skin for long, germs start to breed on them. This produces an unpleasant body odor, which disappears completely when you wash.

You must take extra care over your hygiene in the teens. This diagram shows you the areas for special attention.

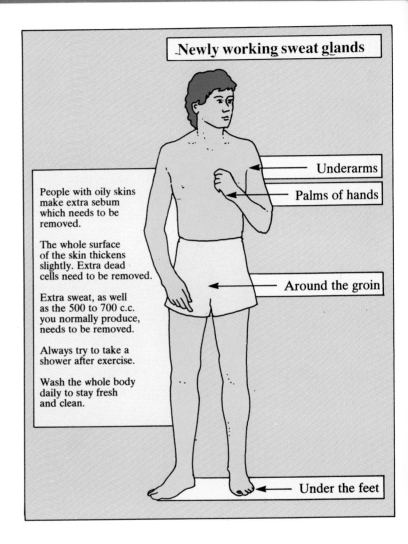

Newly working sweat glands

People with oily skins make extra sebum which needs to be removed.

The whole surface of the skin thickens slightly. Extra dead cells need to be removed.

Extra sweat, as well as the 500 to 700 c.c. you normally produce, needs to be removed.

Always try to take a shower after exercise.

Wash the whole body daily to stay fresh and clean.

Underarms

Palms of hands

Around the groin

Under the feet

During the teens, there may be extra sweating. Extra hygiene is needed to protect your skin from germs that can cause pimples, and to remove the extra sebum, sweat and body oils. Although it is very difficult to prevent pimples altogether, it is possible to make the attacks milder with careful hygiene habits.

HINTS TO HELP

● Use hot water as it softens and melts body oils.

● Use medicated or unscented soap to break down the softened oils.

● If your skin is oily, scrub your back and shoulders with a brush.

● Rinse your skin thoroughly with plenty of clear, cooler water.

● Dry briskly to remove the dead cells and to tone up the skin.

● Scrub nails with a nail-brush. Use a pumice stone on hard patches on the feet.

Using a pumice stone on your feet is a good way of removing hard skin.

If you take care of your clothes, you will always present a neat, pleasing appearance to other people.

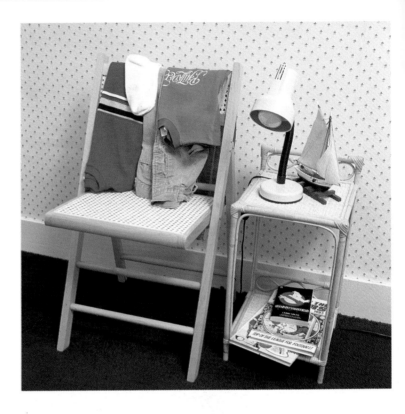

Check your hygiene

Some people spend hours in the bath, and then put on soiled clothes. They wash their face carefully, then forget to clean their teeth. Check your hygiene habits. Guard against a grubby neck, unwashed hair, waxy ears, a dirty nose, sweaty feet or mossy teeth in an otherwise clean body. Build a routine for yourself so you do not forget one particular place.

Clothes that touch your skin pick up some of your body grime. They also mop up some of those millions of dead cells. Underwear, shirts and socks need to be changed daily.

Outer clothes and shoes need to be aired at night, not thrown in a crumpled heap on the floor!

Water

Drink plenty of water. It cleans your insides out and keeps them working well. It puts back the water you lose in sweating. It is very important for your health.

Hands must be washed after using the toilet and before preparing or eating food to guard against passing on, or taking in, germs.

Public signs encourage you to wash your hands after using the toilet, to guard against carrying germs.

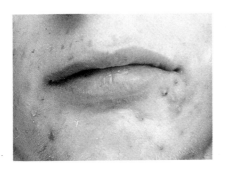

Acne *is a common problem during the teens. It is a very bad attack of pimples. Extra hygiene can help to make attacks milder.*

Stop those pimples!

A bad attack of pimples is called **acne**. The most usual places are the forehead, the sides of the nose, the jaw line and the chin. Acne can also spread to the neck, shoulders, chest and back. Most people have at least one attack in their teens. Over half of all boys aged 14 to 18 have some acne. It is less usual in girls, though they may get more pimples around the time of their monthly period.

WHAT CAUSES ACNE?

1. The extra sebum, sweat and dead cells form a greasy layer on the skin. This attracts dirt and germs, causing pimples.
2. Sebum can be trapped under the slightly thickened skin. It hardens, forming solid little plugs with tops that go black. These are called blackheads.
3. Some people like to pick their pimples. They do this with dirty fingers on dirty skin. They carry the infection all over their face. They actually make their pimples far worse!

How to prevent pimples
Wash that greasy layer from your face at least twice a day.

During the teens, the back sometimes becomes oily and develops pimples. Take care to wash this area to prevent this from happening.

1. Start by washing your hands thoroughly.
2. Use a medicated or unscented soap.
3. Work up a thick lather with your hands and massage it over your face for a full minute.
4. Rinse with scoops of cold water as this helps to close the pores.
5. Brisk drying should be used only if you have heavy oily skin.
6. Delicate skin and pimply places should be dried by gentle patting instead.

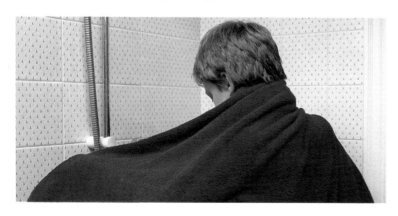

Towel dry your body briskly if you have oily skin. Be gentle on areas where pimples have already formed.

This washing routine should be started at the beginning of the teens. It is often not done until pimples start to show up. Even then, it is not always done regularly. People get bored if they do not see an immediate improvement. They do not realize that this is long-term treatment and must be continued right through the teens. It takes a long time for your hormones to settle down. Pimples are likely to appear if you stop the treatment.

This young surfer is the picture of health as a result of a healthy diet and plenty of exercise outdoors.

How to cope with pimples

1. Dab the pimples with a mild antiseptic lotion on cotton. Remember to use a fresh piece for each pimple or you will spread the infection.
2. Skin treatments may help, but none of them will actually stop you from getting more pimples.
3. Washing and skin treatments can make your skin very dry. Put a little light cream on the dry patches.
4. Sunlight often helps to clear up pimples. Be outdoors when you can. But sunlight ages the skin, so do not stay in the sun too long.
5. Diet is often blamed for teenage pimples, especially fried foods and chocolate. Try to eat more fruit and vegetables.
6. Drink plenty of water to improve the skin, at least four glasses each day.
7. Try never to touch pimples.

Get used to eating fresh fruit from an early age. It will help to keep your skin clear and glowing.

When to go to the doctor

As a single acne pimple heals, it leaves a purplish mark that soon fades. But very infected pimples can take weeks to heal and may leave tiny permanent scars. Go to the doctor if your acne seems to be getting worse. **Antibiotics** are the usual treatment. They can take months to work, so you must be patient. There are now very powerful drugs you may be given. Sadly, they have nasty side effects. If you are using them, follow the instructions carefully. Never share them with a friend. You could be the cause of a great deal of damage.

You can see the blonde down on the forearm of a teenage girl. Boys usually have heavier hair growth on their bodies.

When you wash your hair, work up a rich lather and massage it into your scalp.

Hair

There is no hair on the lips, eyelids, palms and soles of the feet. The rest of the body is covered with **down**, hair so fine and soft it can hardly be seen. Down grows heavier and darker in places, especially during the teens. If you have a rich head of hair, you are likely to have heavier hair on your body too.

Hygiene of the hair

On page 7, you can see the hair growing in its root. Notice the sebaceous gland that makes sebum to oil each separate hair. During the teens, hair can become greasy very quickly. Dead cells from the scalp (head skin) and dirt from the air clings to the grease. The hair smells unfresh and looks unattractive. Wash your hair often. Use a mild shampoo to break down the grease. Rinse the hair in lots of tepid water (warm, not hot) to bring back the gloss.

Hair grows at most openings of the body. Wash under the arms and around the groin daily. Hair in the ears and nose trap dirt. Make sure you clean them daily too. Tiny glands make oil for the eyelashes. This oil can harden into tiny crusts. Soften the crusts with baby oil until they come away by themselves. Remove any "sleep" or dirt from the corner of your eyes gently with damp cotton.

Dandruff

During the teens, more dead skin cells flake off the scalp. You may notice white patches in your hair or on your shoulders. This is called dandruff. It is harmless; you cannot pass it on, nor catch it. But it looks unattractive, and there is a risk the scalp can become infected if too much oil sticks to the dandruff. Wash your hair more often. Use a dandruff treatment shampoo. Brush your hair first to loosen the scales.

Hair care

1. Wash your brush and comb each time you wash your hair.
2. Try not to borrow brushes and combs. If you do, wash them before returning.
3. Hair can split or break off at the ends. Trim the ends regularly. Make sure this is not caused by over-hot curling or straightening. Tints and bleaches can also damage the hair.

Lice

Lice are tiny creatures that live in human hair. They have curved claws to give them a firm grip. They pierce the skin and suck up blood. The skin becomes sore and very itchy. DO NOT SCRATCH IT!

The head louse is common among children.

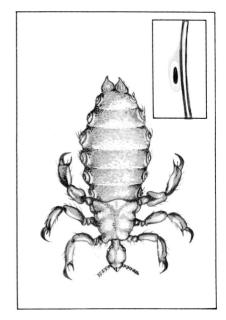

A head louse uses sharp claws to pierce the scalp and feed off the blood. The inset shows a nit *attached to a hair.*

If you develop head lice, use the special lotion and ask somebody to check your hair with a nit comb as shown here.

though older people can catch them. Body lice can live in the hair around the groin. The female louse lays about sixty eggs called **nits** each month. She glues each nit to the hair with a strong cement. The nit hatches out in a week, and is fully grown in three weeks.

Anyone can catch lice. They crawl from person to person where the hair is in close contact. Usually, a whole family will be infected. Head lice can be removed with a special lotion and a nit comb bought from the pharmacist. The treatment must be repeated until all the nits are removed. Body lice need to be treated by the doctor.

Having lice is bad luck. It does not mean you are "dirty." You have caught them from someone else. It is likely you have already passed them on to other people too. There is nothing to be ashamed of. Tell the principal of your school so that the infection can be cleared up quickly.

Boils

Boils are caused by germs that infect the hair root. They grow much larger than acne pimples and can be quite painful. The first sign is a red swelling that may be itchy. Keep the whole area clean. Never try to squeeze a boil. Go to the doctor for treatment and a check-up on your general health. It is important to get treatment to stop more boils from developing.

A boil can be quite painful. It is caused by a single hair root being infected by germs.

Your hands and feet

Nails are made from special skin cells. They begin to grow half way back to the first joint of the finger. The cells here are very sensitive. A really hard blow can damage the cells. They produce extra layers, so there is a thick, horny lump. This grows out in about three to six months. A mild blow can cause a blood blister under the nail.

Keep your nails clean by scrubbing them with a nail-brush.

Care of the cuticles

The **cuticle** is the rim of skin around the nail bed. It acts as a seal, keeping germs out. Most cuticles do not need to be pushed back. Proper drying of the fingers, from the tips downward, should keep them in place. Hangnails are bits of torn cuticle. Do not bite or pull them off. Cut them down with fine scissors. If the raw edges keep snagging, cover them with a bandage while they heal.

A **whitlow** is an infection on or near the cuticle. It must be treated by a doctor. Any infection around the nail needs medical treatment as there is a risk of germs getting under the nail bed and causing damage.

Are you a nail-biter?

Nail-biters enjoy biting their nails. This makes the habit difficult to stop. It generally stops as people get older. It is not dangerous to health, but it looks unattractive. Some nail-biters are slightly anxious people. If you are, think about taking up **yoga**. Try to get more sleep.

Cutting the nails

Toenails should be cut straight across in short little snips. This stops the nail from bending. Toenails can be cut after a bath when the nail is soft. Do not cut down the sides of the nails. This can cause a painful condition called **ingrown toenails**. Young people sometimes forget to cut their toenails, which grow into long claws and curl under the toes.

Care of the feet

Shoes should protect the feet, not deform them.

Bitten nails are very unattractive. If you bite your nails, it can be a sign that you are overanxious. Try to exercise more to help work off worried feelings.

Any shoe that feels tight or rubs the foot can twist it out of shape. Study the picture. That person once had perfect feet! Now, the toes are deformed and covered with corns. There is a bunion at the side of the foot. Walking is quite painful. Will you choose to let all these things happen to your feet?

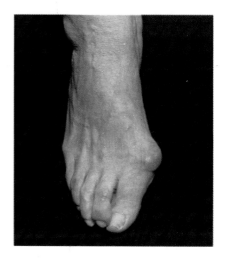

Ill-fitting shoes deform the feet. The corns and bunion on this foot are the result of wearing tight-fitting shoes that rubbed and stopped the foot from growing properly.

HINTS TO HELP

● Buy shoes that allow room for growth.
● Both feet must be measured. One foot is often larger than the other.
● Try on both shoes. Walk around. Stand on tip-toe. Shoes must be comfortable.
● Socks should be loose around the toes, or they can deform the feet too. They are best made of cotton or wool, as natural fibers let the feet "breathe."
● Walk around barefoot whenever you can.

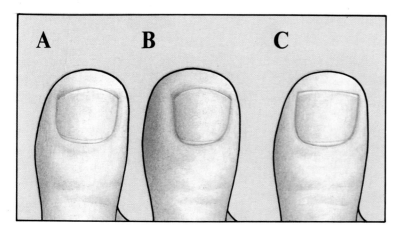

*Ingrown toenails (**B**) are caused when people do not cut their toenails correctly (see **A**). Be sure to cut straight across the nail (see **C**).*

Ringworm – athlete's foot

There are no worms in **ringworm**. It is a skin infection caused by a **fungus** that spreads out into a ring. Small children may get ringworm infection of the scalp. In the teens, ringworm on the upper leg or the feet, which is called athlete's foot, is more usual.

You can catch ringworm whether you are athletic or not! Ringworm is very **infectious**. It is passed by contact (direct touch), for example, sharing towels and sports gear, especially shoes. It can also be picked up from the floors of gyms or locker rooms. Boys seem to catch it more often than girls, especially during warm weather.

Signs of ringworm

On the feet, small cracks appear between the toes. The cracks open, the skin turns whitish and

Be careful when you are in a locker room to guard against picking up infections. Do not use other peoples towels or gear.

"weeps." Then it peels off leaving raw, red patches that are itchy. Or it may start as small yellow blisters under the feet. They spread to the heels and make them sore.

Ringworm of the leg begins high up near the groin on the inside of the leg. There is a small red, slightly bumpy patch on the skin. The patch grows and spreads down the inside thigh for 5 to 7 mm. It looks rather nasty, but it is not dangerous to health.

It takes time and patience to get rid of ringworm. You need treatment from your doctor. You must take extra care with your hygiene so that:

> a) you do not pass the infection to other people.
> b) you do not infect other parts of your own skin.

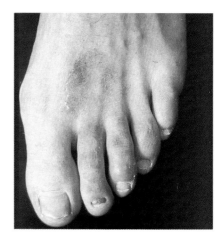

Athlete's foot is a form of ringworm common among teenagers. Take extra care to keep your feet clean, and always dry them thoroughly.

HINTS TO HELP

● Do not borrow or lend sports gear, shoes or towels. Keep them clean.
● Always use the footbaths in a public swimming pool.
● After exercise, wash your skin thoroughly with plenty of soap and warm water.
● Rinse your skin really well before drying, then put on your clean clothes and shoes.

Keeping clean and looking good

Cuts and scratches: The skin acts as a barrier to stop germs from getting in. When the skin is broken open there is a risk of infection from germs, and care must be taken. Cuts can be held under cold running water to wash out the germs and to slow the bleeding. Dab a little antiseptic on the cut to kill off any germs.

Tiny cuts heal quickly if they are left open to the fresh air. The ultraviolet rays in sunlight kill off many germs. Larger cuts need to be covered with a bandage while the healing scab forms.

Cover large cuts with a bandage to stop germs from getting in. Leave it on until the scab forms.

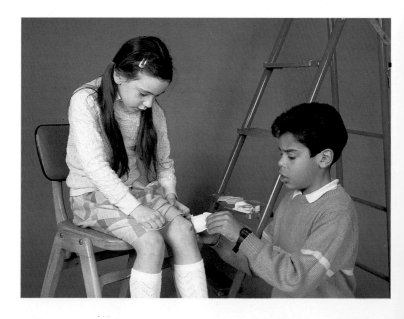

The bandage stops new germs from getting in, and prevents any infection from the cut spreading to other people.

Posture: Are you sitting up straight? Do you "walk tall"? Bones grow strong and healthy when they are held in the right place.

Teeth: When you smile, do you show a lovely set of teeth? Visit your dentist regularly. Use **fluoride** toothpaste and dental floss to keep your teeth healthy and your breath sweet.

Brush your teeth regularly and always rinse your mouth out thoroughly afterward.

Remember to brush up and down, rather than from just side to side. Brush your gums too, to guard against gum disease later on.

Expression: Do you smile often? Are your eyes bright and alert? If not, have your eyesight checked for any problems. And make sure you get enough sleep. In the teens, you need more sleep, not less. The growth hormone works best while you are asleep.

Try to get plenty of sleep during the teens. This will help your growth hormone *to work better.*

A bright, alert expression, glossy hair and clear skin will always make you attractive to other people and give you confidence.

Looks and health

The way you look partly depends on how healthy you are inside. If your diet is poor or you get little exercise, then you will not feel or look healthy, no matter how much time you spend on your appearance. Try to eat more fruit and vegetables and eat less fatty foods and sweets. Your skin will benefit greatly. Remember, take care of your body both inside and outside and you will gain confidence from your healthy, attractive appearance.

Glossary

Acne A very bad attack of pimples.

Antibiotics Medical drugs that work by making the body's own defense system fight an infection.

Cuticle The rim of skin around the nail bed acting as a barrier to keep germs out.

Dandruff Condition caused by dead skin cells flaking off the scalp.

Dermis The deep, inner layer of the skin.

Down The light, soft hair that covers all parts of the body apart from the eyelids, lips, palms of the hands and soles of the feet. This **down** becomes thicker on certain parts of the body when the child is developing into an adult.

Epidermis The thin outer layer of the skin, which is protective.

Fluoride An important substance that helps make your teeth strong and hard.

Fungus Plant-like structure (often tiny) that can multiply very quickly over the surface of the body or plant that provides its nourishment.

Hormones The chemical messengers that control your growth and development.

Infectious If an illness is infectious, this means that it can be caught very easily.

Ingrown toenails A painful condition that comes about when the toenail begins to grow into the skin at the side of the toe.

Lice Tiny creatures that live in human hair. Body **lice** live in the hair around the groin. They pierce the skin and suck up blood.

Nits The eggs that the female louse (plural **lice**) lays each month in the hair. Each **nit** is glued to the hair with a strong cement, hatches out in a week and is fully grown in three weeks.

Ringworm A skin complaint caused by a **fungus** spreading outward in a circle and becoming red, slightly bumpy and itchy. When it affects the feet, it is called athlete's foot.

Sebaceous glands Structures beneath the skin that produce the oil called **sebum**.

Sebum The special oil produced to keep your skin smooth and waterproof and your hair glossy.

Sweat gland One of thousands of tiny, coiled tube-like structures under the skin that produce **sweat**. This consists of water and some of the waste products from the body.

Whitlow An infection on or near the **cuticle**.

Yoga A course of exercises that help people to learn how to relax by breathing deeply and stretching and holding their bodies in certain set positions.

© Copyright 1987 Wayland (Publishers) Ltd
61 Western Road, Hove, East Sussex BN3 1JD, England

Further reading

If you would like to find out more about how your body works and how to be healthy, you might like to read the following books:

Kozuszek, Jane Eyerly. *Hygiene*. Watts, 1978.

McCoy, Kathy. *The Teenage Body Book*. Simon & Schuster, 1984.

Madaras, Lynda. *What's Happening To My Body? A Growing Up Guide For Mothers And Daughters*. Newmarket Press, 1983.

Madaras, Lynda. *What's Happening To My Body? Book For Boys: A Growing Up Guide For Parents And Sons*. Newmarket Press, 1984.

Stiller, Richard. *Your Body Is Trying To Tell You Something: How To Understand Its Signals And Respond To Its Needs*. Harcourt, 1979.

Picture acknowledgments

The Publisher would like to thank the following for providing pictures for this book: Andrew Popkiewicz 8, 23; Cameratalks 14, 20 (both), 23, 25; Malcolm Walker 7, 10, 19; Sporting Pictures (UK) Ltd 9; Tim Woodcock cover, 5 (both), 11, 12, 13, 15 (both), 18 (below), 21, 22; Tropix 18 (above), 29; Zefa 4, 6, 17, 27, 28. The remainder are from the Wayland Picture Library.

Index

Acne 14, 17
Antibiotics 17
Antiseptic lotion 16, 26
Appearance 4, 5, 12, 29
Athlete's foot 24–5

Body 18
    fluids 8, 9
    odor 5, 9
    oils 8, 9, 10, 11, 18
Boils 20
Breath 5, 27
Bunions 23

Cells 11, 14, 18
Clothes 5, 7, 12, 13, 25
Confidence 5, 29
Corns 23
Cuts 26, 27
Cuticles 21–2

Damp 4, 8, 9
Dandruff 6, 19
Dermis 7
Diet 4, 16, 29
Disease 28
Doctor 17, 20, 22
Down 18
Drying 11, 15, 21, 25

Ears 8, 12, 18
Epidermis 7
Exercise 4, 8, 22, 25, 29

Expression 5, 28, 29
Eyes 5, 8, 18, 19, 28

Feet 11, 12, 18, 21
    22, 23, 24, 25
Fungus 24

Genitals 8
Germs 4, 9, 10, 13, 14
    20, 21, 22, 26, 27
Glands 8, 18
Grease 14, 18
Gums 28

Habits 4, 12
Hair 5, 8, 12, 18
    19, 20, 29
    care 8, 18, 19
Hormones 6, 16
    growth 6, 28

Infections 14, 16, 19, 20,
    22, 24, 25, 26, 27
Ingrown toenails 22, 23

Lice 19–20

Mucus 8

Nails 4, 5, 11, 21, 22
Nail-biting 4, 22
Nits 19–20

Pimples 6, 10, 14, 15, 16,
    17
Posture 5, 27

Ringworm 24–5

Scalp 18, 19, 24
Sebum 8, 10, 14, 18
Shampoo 18, 19
Shoes 13, 22–3, 24, 25
Shyness 8
Skin 4, 5, 7, 8, 9, 10, 12,
    15, 16, 17, 19, 24, 25,
    26, 29
    cells 7, 11, 12, 14, 19,
        21
    oily 8, 11, 14, 15
Sleep 22, 28
Soap 10, 11, 15, 25
Sweat 8, 9, 10, 12, 13, 14

Tears 8
Teens 6, 7, 8, 10, 14, 15,
    16, 18, 19, 24, 25, 28
Teeth 5, 12, 27–8
Towels 15, 24, 25

Water 11, 13, 15, 16, 18,
    25–6
Wax 8, 12
Whitlow 22

Yoga 22